French Knot — Follow numbers in Diagram G to bring needle up at 1. Wind floss once around needle and take needle down at 2, holding loose end of floss tight until knot is formed.

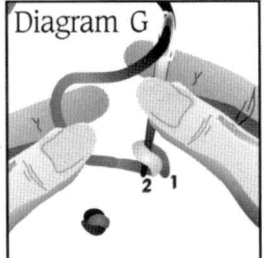

Beads — Add beads after stitching is complete. Follow numbers in Diagram H to b...

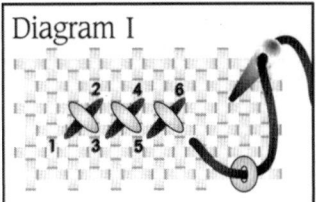

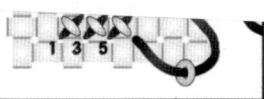

Run the floss through the bead and take needle down at 2. When working over two threads on linen or similar fabrics, follow numbers in Diagram I.

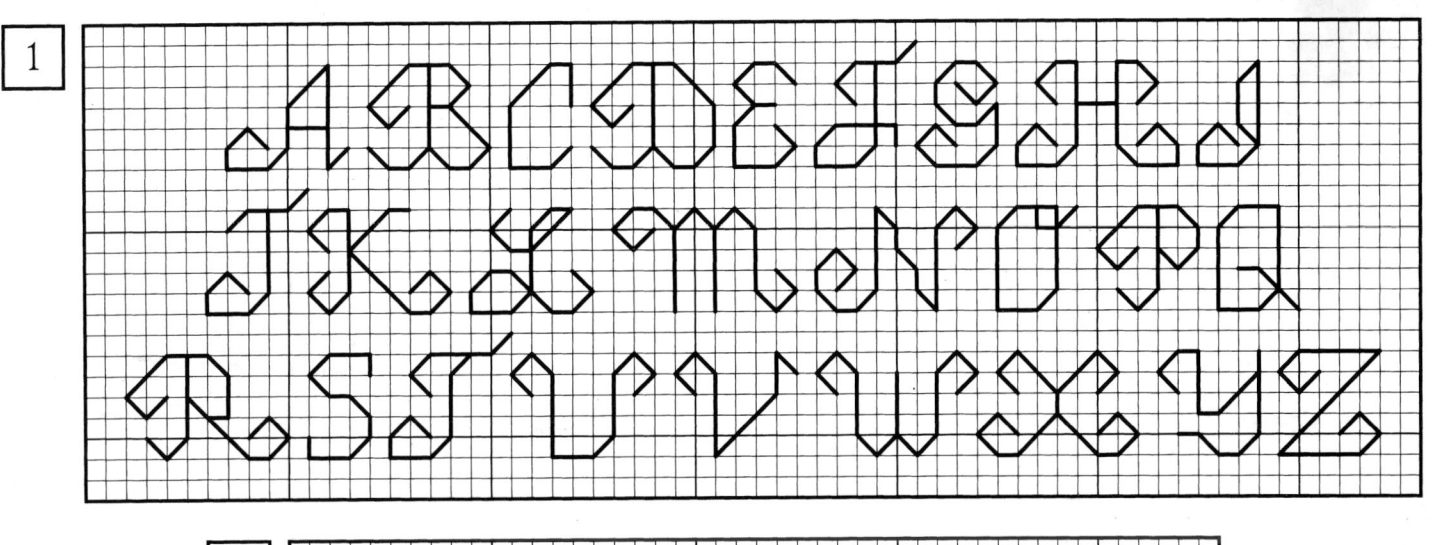

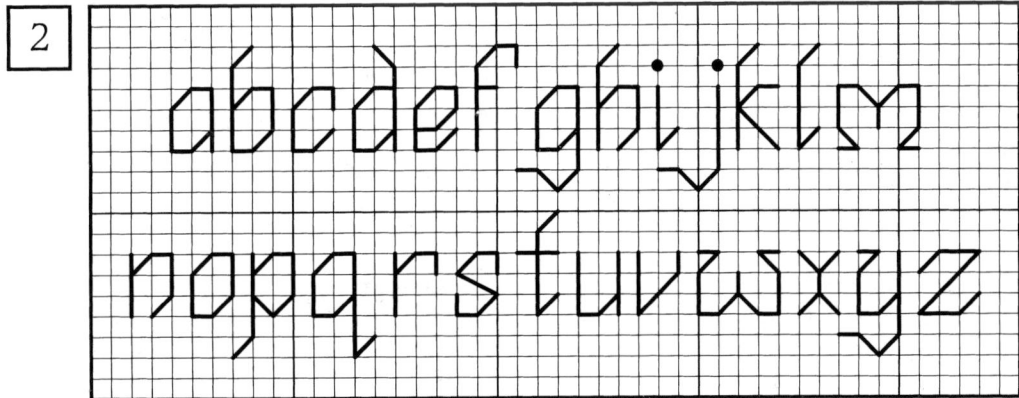

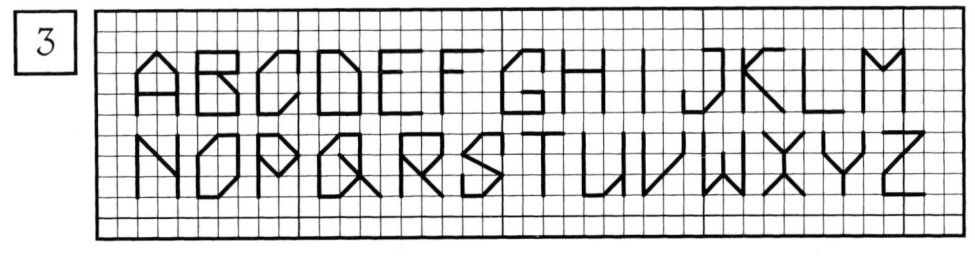

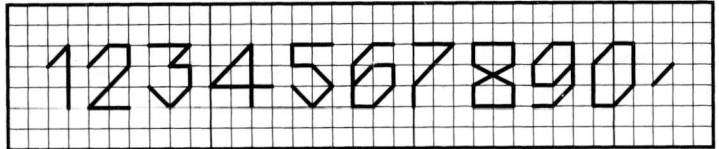

The information in this book is presented in good faith; however, no warranty is given, nor are results guaranteed. Praying Hands disclaims any liability for untoward results. The designs in this book are protected by copyright and are not to be used for commercial sales or reproduction; however, you may make the designs for your personal use or to sell for pin money.

Designs by Mary Scott.

© 1996 Praying Hands
P.O. Box 55086, Little Rock, AR 72215
Printed in the United States of America

IF WE LOVE ONE ANOTHER

Stitch Count:
57 wide x 61 high

Project Information: The design was stitched on a 10¼" x 10½" piece of 28 count Cream Cashel Linen® over two fabric threads. It was custom framed.

Cross Stitch – 3 strands

Symbol	Color	DMC	Anchor
=	mauve	316	1017
■	lt mauve	778	968
♥	dk green	3362	263
$	green	3363	262
✓	dk mauve	3726	1018

Backstitch – 1 strand

Symbol	Color
╱	dk green for thorns
╱	green for remaining backstitch

French Knot – 1 strand

Symbol	Color
•	green

AND THE TWO SHALL BECOME ONE

Stitch Count:
85 wide x 115 high

Project Information: The design was stitched on a 12¼" x 14¼" piece of 28 count Cream Cashel Linen® over two fabric threads. It was custom framed. To personalize design, use one strand of dk green and refer to alphabet 3 and numbers, page 2.

Cross Stitch – 3 strands

Symbol	Color	DMC	Anchor
■	mauve	316	1017
•	green	522	860
▼	lt green	523	859
▨	lt mauve	778	968
$	dk green	3363	262
⬠	dk mauve	3726	1018

Backstitch – 1 strand

Symbol	Color
╱	dk mauve

French Knot – 1 strand

Symbol	Color
•	dk mauve

Beads

Symbol	Color
⊕	Mill Hill Glass Seed Bead #00151 ash mauve
⊙	Mill Hill Glass Seed Bead #00553 old rose

AND THEY SHALL BECOME ONE FLESH

Stitch Count: 79 wide x 56 high

Project Information: The design was stitched on an 11¾" x 10" piece of 28 count Cream Cashel Linen® over two fabric threads. It was custom framed.

Cross Stitch – 3 strands

Symbol	Color	DMC	Anchor
+	mauve	316	1017
☆	lt green	522	860
◉	lt mauve	778	968
♥	green	3362	263
■	dk mauve	3726	1018

Backstitch – 1 strand

Symbol	Color
∕	green for leaves
∕	dk mauve for remaining backstitch

French Knot – 1 strand

Symbol	Color
●	dk mauve

Beads

Symbol	Color
○	Mill Hill Glass Seed Bead #02012 royal plum

LOVE ONE ANOTHER WITH A PURE HEART

Stitch Count: 87 wide x 111 high

Project Information: The design was stitched on a 12¼" x 14" piece of 28 count Cream Cashel Linen® over two fabric threads. It was custom framed. To personalize design, use two strands of dk blue grey and refer to alphabets 1, 2, and numbers, page 2.

Cross Stitch – 3 strands

Symbol	Color	DMC	Anchor
·	white	blanc	2
■	mauve	316	1017
■	lt green	524	858
◉	lt mauve	778	968
✱	dk blue grey	926	850
=	blue grey	927	848
❖	green	3363	262
‖	dk mauve	3726	1018

Backstitch

Symbol	Color
∕	mauve for flowers - 1 strand
∕	dk blue grey for Scripture and Reference - 1 strand
∕	lt green for stems - 2 strands
∕	blue grey for running stitch - 2 strands

French Knot – 1 strand

Symbol	Color
●	dk blue grey

Beads

Symbol	Color
○	Mill Hill Glass Seed Bead #00553 old rose

THIS IS MY BELOVED

Stitch Count: 95 wide x 123 high

Project Information: The design was stitched on a 13" x 15" piece of 28 count Cream Cashel Linen® over two fabric threads. It was custom framed. To personalize design, use one strand of blue grey and refer to alphabet 3 and numbers, page 2.

Cross Stitch – 3 strands

Symbol	Color	DMC	Anchor
■	mauve	316	1017
·	lt green	524	858
═	lt mauve	778	968
◊	blue grey	926	850
✚	green	3363	262

Cross Stitch – 3 strands

Symbol	Color	DMC	Anchor
▨	dk mauve	3726	1018

Backstitch

Symbol	Color
╱	blue grey - 2 strands

Backstitch

Symbol	Color
╱	blue grey - 1 strand

French Knot – 1 strand

Symbol	Color
•	blue grey

Shaded area indicates last row stitched on bottom section.

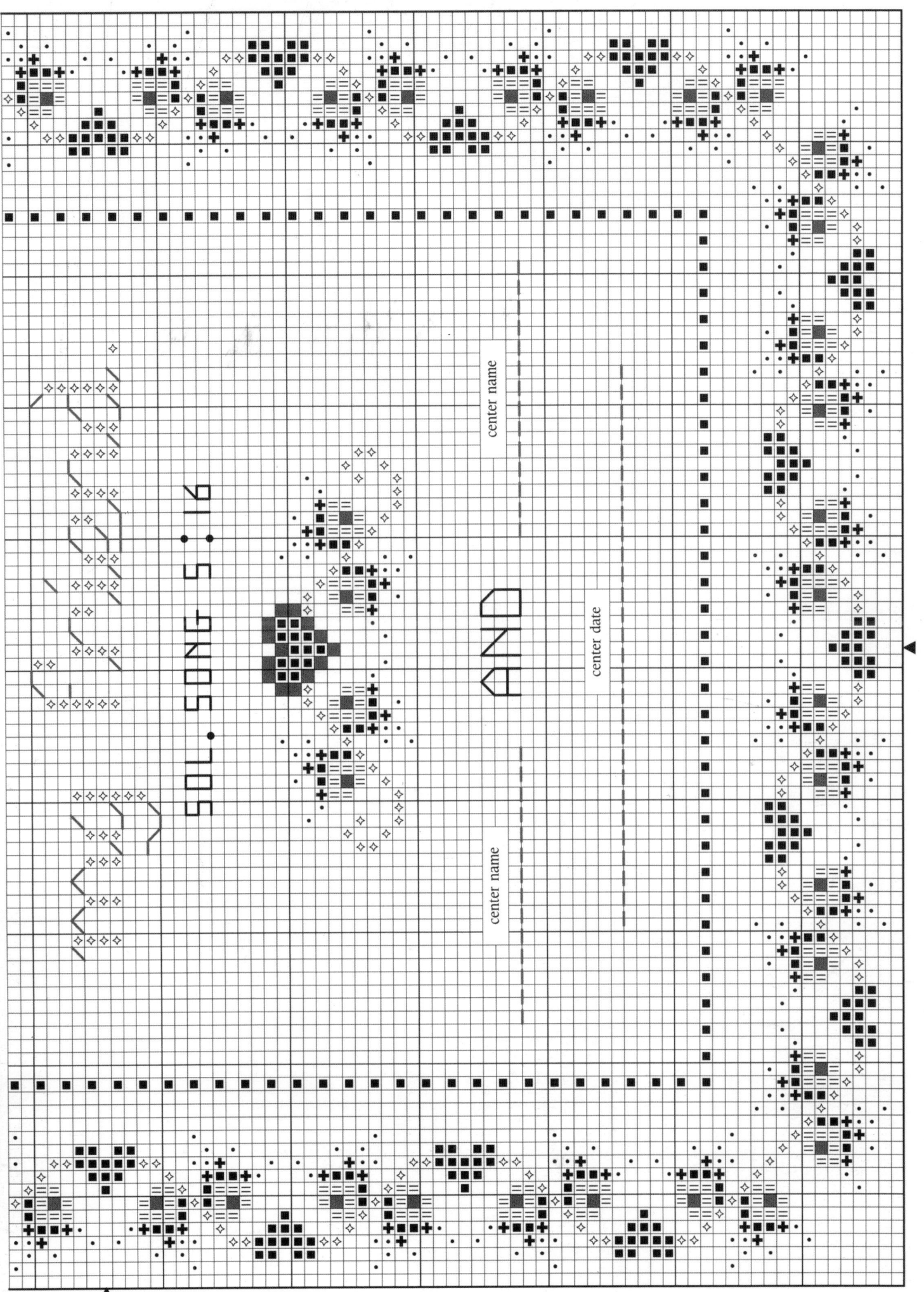

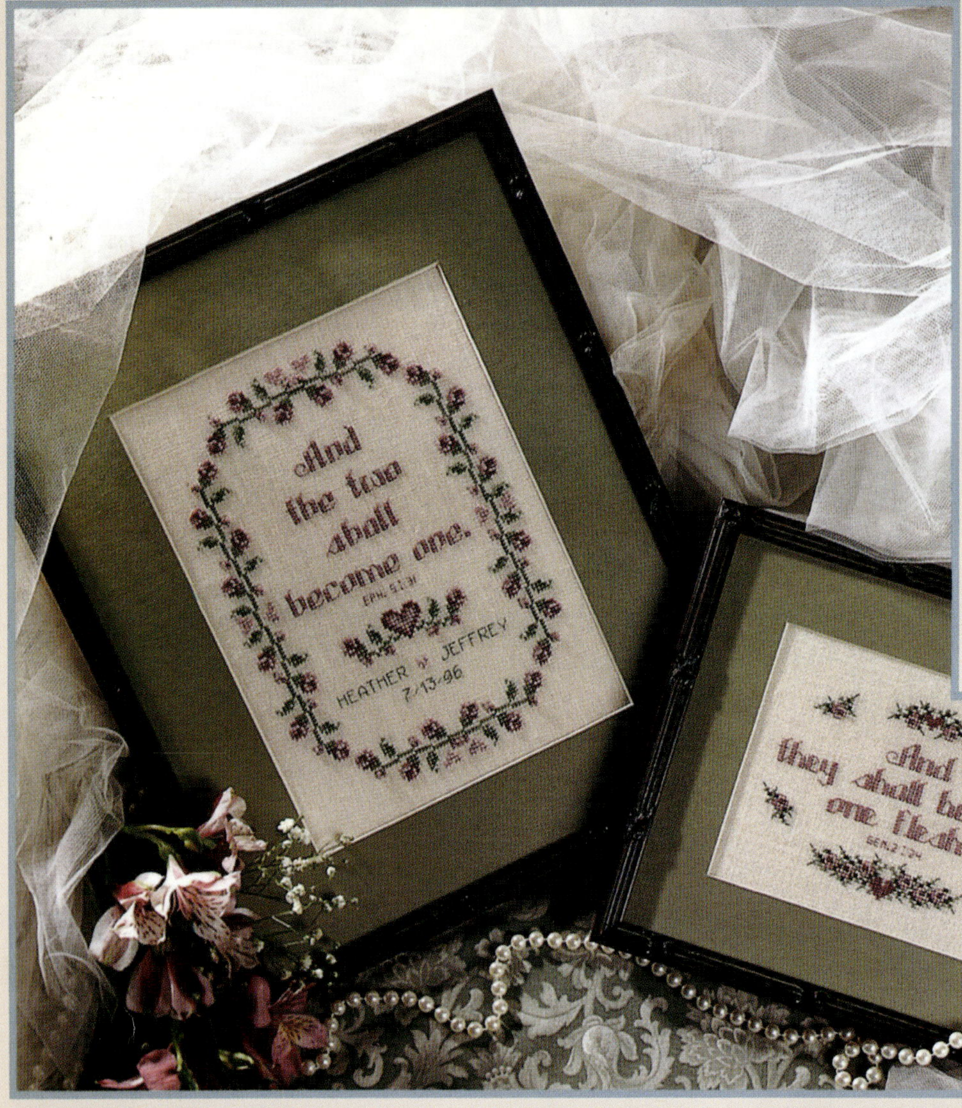
And the two shall become one.
And they shall become one flesh.

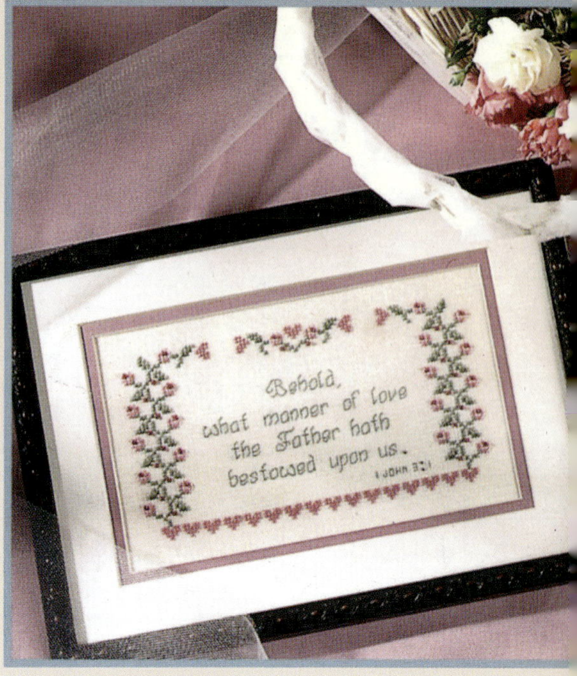
Behold, what manner of love the Father hath bestowed upon us.

Behold, how good and pleasant it is to dwell together in unity.

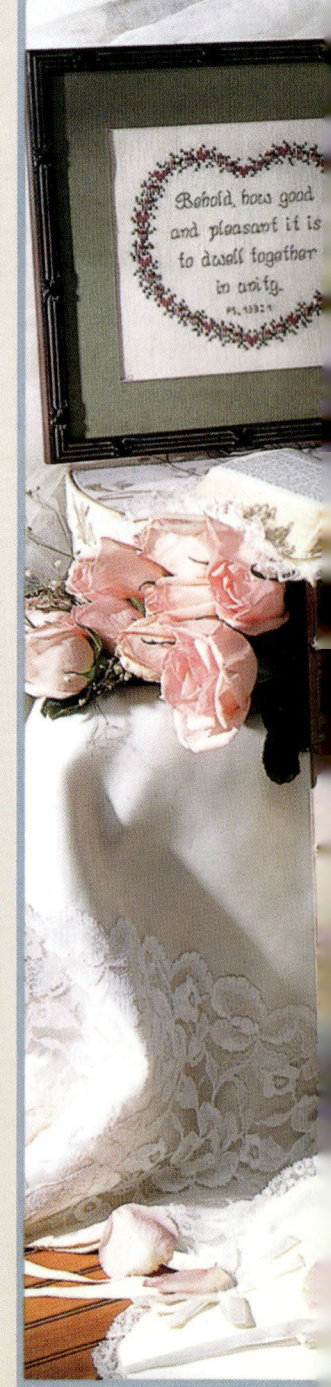

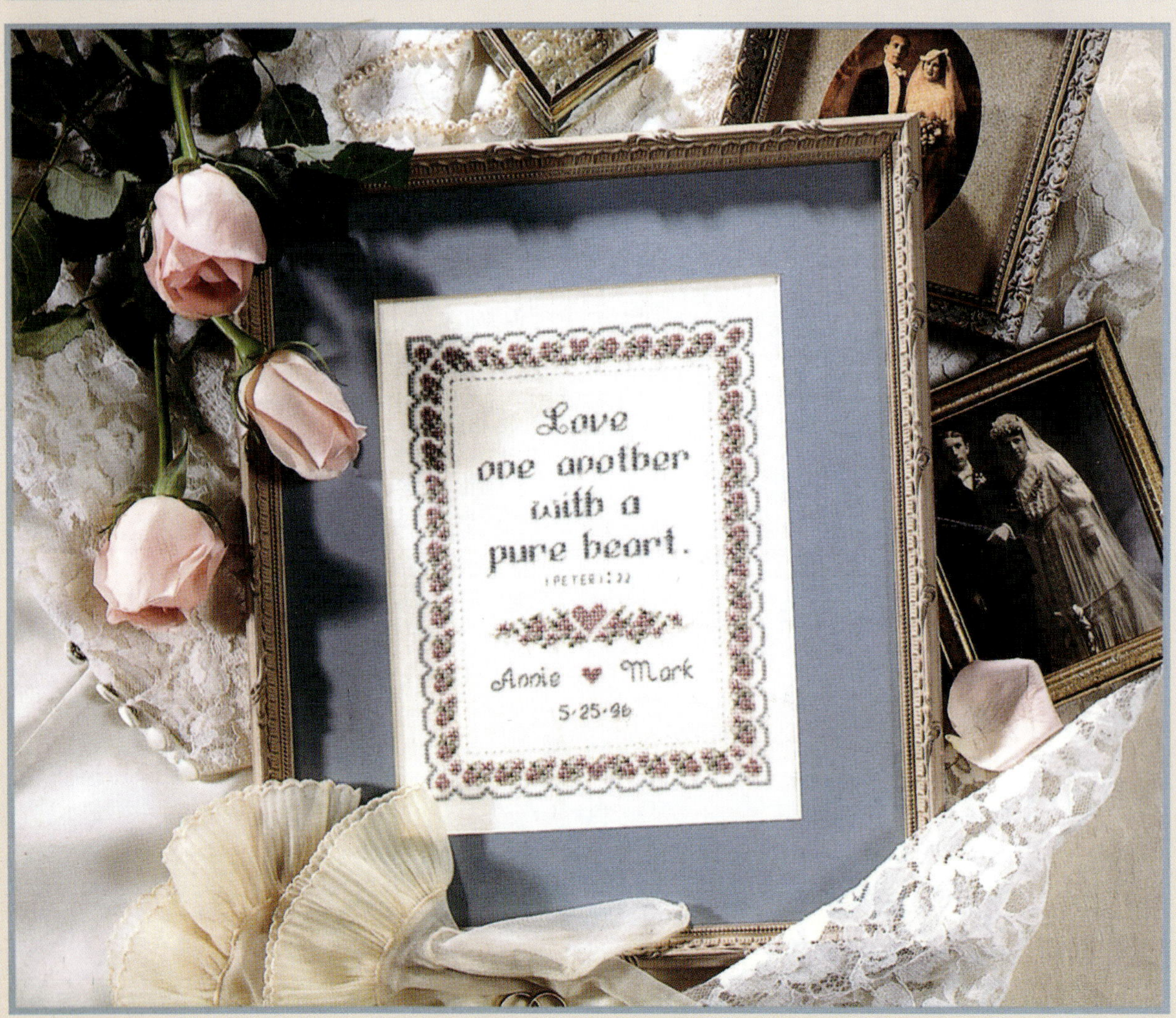
Love one another with a pure heart.
Annie Mark
5-25-96

LOVE IS PATIENT

Stitch Count: 123 wide x 159 high

Project Information: The design was stitched on a 15" x 17½" piece of 28 count Cream Cashel Linen® over two fabric threads. It was custom framed. To personalize design, use dk green and refer to alphabet 3 and numbers, page 2.

Cross Stitch – 3 strands

Symbol	Color	DMC	Anchor
◇	blue grey	926	850
■	lt mauve	3354	74
·	dk green	3362	263
✕	green	3363	262
	mauve	3688	66
	dk mauve	3803	

Backstitch – 1 strand

Symbol	Color
	blue grey for stems
	dk green for Scripture and Reference
	dk mauve for remaining backstitch

French Knot – 1 strand

Symbol	Color
●	dk green

Beads

Symbol	Color
○	Mill Hill Glass Seed Bead #02012 royal plum

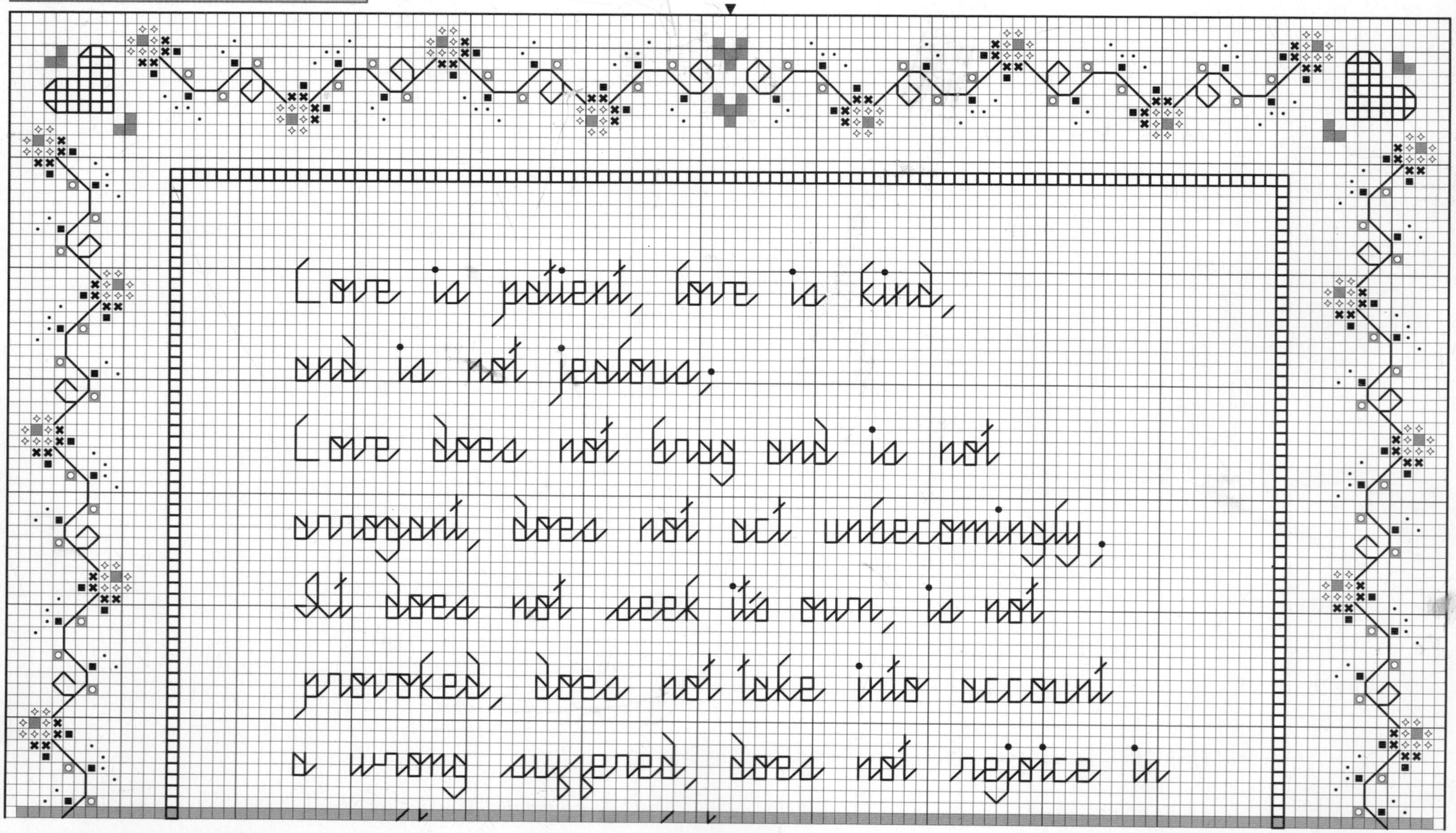

Shaded area indicates last row stitched on bottom section.

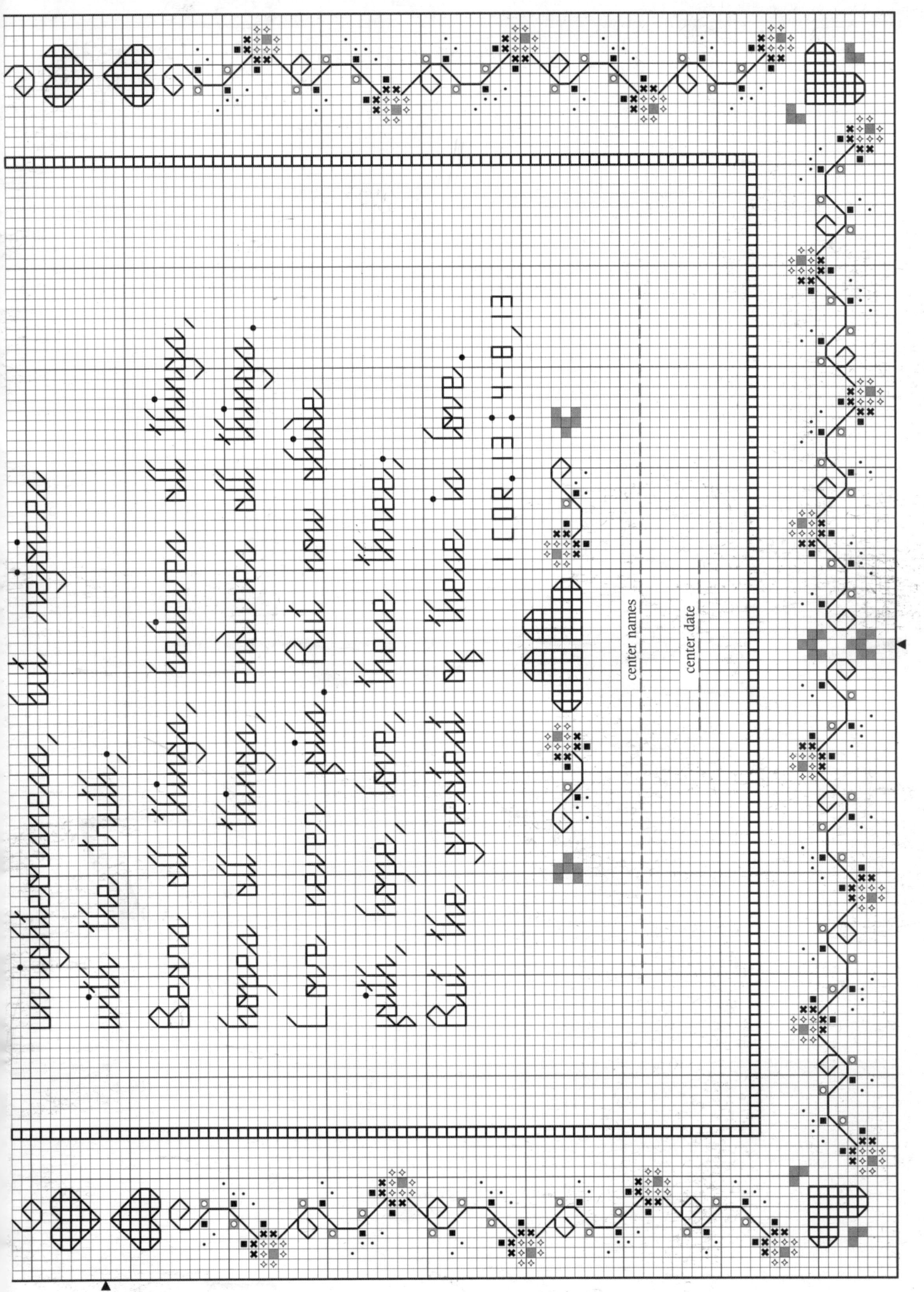

FOR WHITHER THOU GOEST

Stitch Count: 123 wide x 149 high

Project Information: The design was stitched on a 15" x 16¾" piece of 28 count Cream Cashel Linen® over two fabric threads. It was custom framed. To personalize design, use green and refer to alphabets 1, 2, and numbers, page 2.

Cross Stitch – 3 strands

Symbol	Color	DMC	Anchor
X	lt green	522	860
H	lt mauve	3354	74
◣	green	3362	263
▨	dk mauve	3687	68
◁	mauve	3688	66

Backstitch – 1 strand

Symbol	Color
╱	green

French Knot – 1 strand

Symbol	Color
•	green

Beads

Symbol	Color
◉	Mill Hill Glass Seed Bead #02012 royal plum

For whither thou goest,
I will go;
And where thou lodgest,
I will lodge;
Thy people shall be

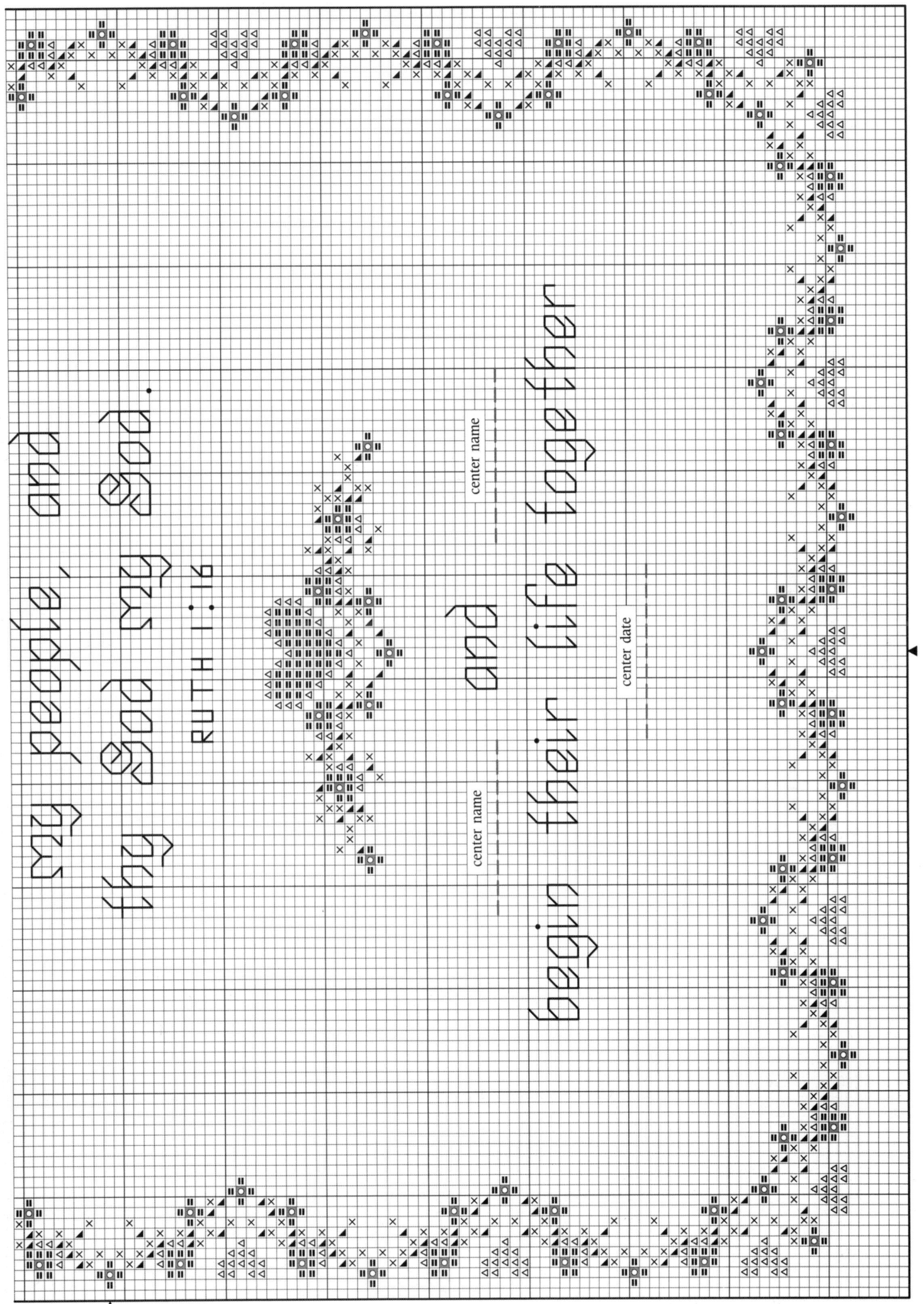

BEHOLD, HOW GO

Stitch Count:
87 wide x 71 high

Project Information: The design was stitched on a 12¼" x 11¼" piece of 28 count Cream Cashel Linen® over two fabric threads. It was custom framed.

Cross Stitch – 3 strands

Symbol	Color	DMC	Anchor
•	mauve	316	1017
✕	lt green	523	859
═	lt mauve	778	968
	green	3363	262
✳	pink	3687	68
◤	dk mauve	3803	

Backstitch – 1 strand

Symbol	Color
✓	green

French Knot – 1 strand

Symbol	Color
•	green

Beads

Symbol	Color
○	Mill Hill Glass Seed Bead #02012 royal plum

15

LOVE ONE ANOTHER AS I HAVE LOVED YOU

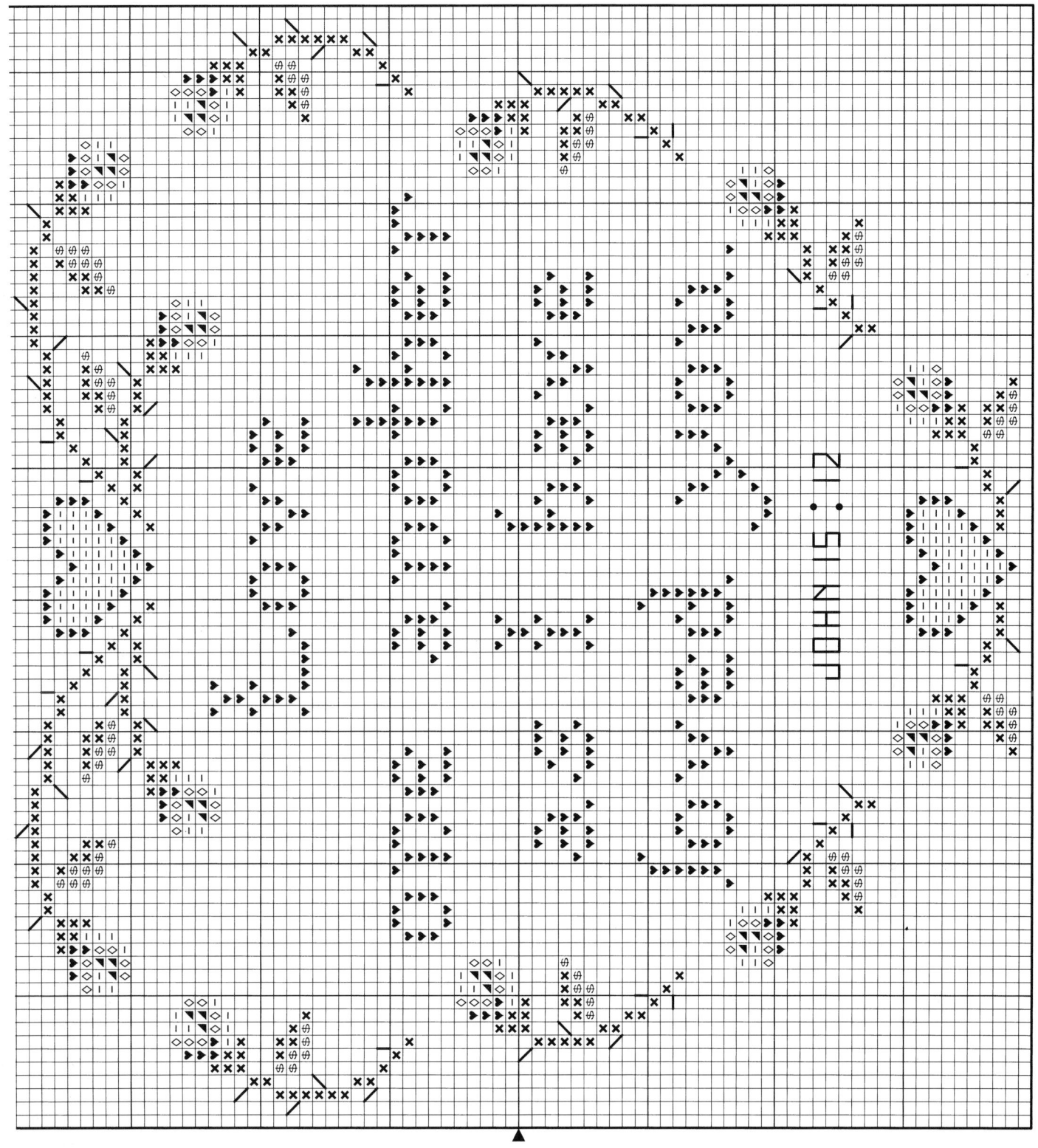

Stitch Count:
83 wide x 78 high

Project Information: The design was stitched on a 12" x 11³/₄" piece of 28 count Cream Cashel Linen® over two fabric threads. It was custom framed.

Cross Stitch – 3 strands

Symbol	Color	DMC	Anchor
$	dk green	3362	263
x	green	3363	262
▶	mauve	3687	68
–	lt mauve	3688	66
◇	vy lt mauve	3689	49
◣	dk mauve	3803	

Backstitch – 1 strand

Symbol	Color
╱	dk green for thorns
╱	mauve for remaining backstitch

French Knot – 1 strand

Symbol	Color
•	mauve

YE SHALL ABIDE

Stitch Count:
93 wide x 93 high

Project Information: The design was stitched on a 12¾" x 12¾" piece of 28 count Cream Cashel Linen® over two fabric threads. It was custom framed. To personalize design, use two strands of dk blue grey and refer to alphabets 1, 2, and numbers, page 2.

Cross Stitch - 3 strands

Symbol	Color	DMC	Anchor
■	mauve	316	1017
✕	lt green	522	860
−	lt mauve	778	968
☆	dk blue grey	926	850
•	blue grey	927	848
◢	green	3362	263
■	dk mauve	3726	1018

French Knot - 1 strand

Symbol	Color
╱	dk blue grey

Beads

Symbol	Color
○	Mill Hill Glass Seed Bead #00553 old rose